"We travel not to escape life, but for life not to escape us."

—Anonymous

www.ingramcontent.com/pod-product-compliance
Lightning Source LLC
Chambersburg PA
CBHW031623210526
45464CB00004B/1716
*9781982968441*